Virginia
Facts and Symbols

by Bill McAuliffe

Consultant:
Sara B. Bearss
Managing Editor
Virginia Historical Society

Hilltop Books
an imprint of Franklin Watts
A Division of Grolier Publishing
New York   London   Hong Kong   Sydney
Danbury, Connecticut

Hilltop Books
http://publishing.grolier.com

Library of Congress Cataloging-in-Publication Data
McAuliffe, Bill.
   Virginia facts and symbols/by Bill McAuliffe.
   p. cm.—(The states and their symbols)
   Includes bibliographical references and index.
   Summary: Presents information about the state of Virginia, its nickname, motto,
and emblems.
   ISBN 0-7368-0221-5
   1. Emblems, State—Virginia—Juvenile literature. [1. Emblems, State—Virginia.
2. Virginia.] I. Title. II. Series: McAuliffe, Emily. States and their symbols.
CR203.V8M38   1999
975.5—dc21
                                                                98-10893
                                                                CIP
                                                                AC

Editorial Credits
Chuck Miller, editor; Steve Christensen, cover designer; Linda Clavel, illustrator;
   Kimberly Danger, photo researcher

Photo Credits
David Liebman, 16
Kent and Donna Dannen, 6
The Mariners' Museum/John Pemberton, 22 (bottom)
One Mile Up, Inc., 8, 10 (inset)
Photophile/Anthony Merciea, 12
Rainbow/Jeff Greenberg, 10
Rob and Ann Simpson, cover
Robert McCaw, 20
Unicorn Stock Photos/Karen Holsinger Mullen, 14; Robert Hitchman, 22 (top)
William B. Folsom, 18, 22 (middle)

Table of Contents

Fast Facts

Capital: Richmond is the capital of Virginia.

Largest City: Virginia Beach is the largest city in Virginia. More than 430,000 people live in this city.

Size: Virginia covers 40,598 square miles (105,149 square kilometers). It is the 37th-largest state.

Location: Virginia is a southeastern state.

Population: 6,733,996 people live in Virginia (U.S. Census Bureau, 1997 estimate).

Statehood: Virginia became the 10th state to join the United States on June 25, 1788.

Natural Resources: Lumber, fish, and minerals are important natural resources in Virginia.

Manufactured Goods: Virginia's businesses produce clothes, and transportation and electrical equipment.

Crops: Virginia farmers grow soybeans and corn. They also raise beef and dairy cattle.

State Name and Nickname

Virginia was named in honor of Queen Elizabeth I of England. She was known as the Virgin Queen. In 1497, English explorer John Cabot sailed to North America. He discovered the land now known as Virginia. The English later claimed the region for their queen. They named it Virginia in her honor.

Virginia's nickname is the Old Dominion. A dominion is a colony that is allowed to govern itself. King Charles II of England called Virginia one of his dominions.

Virginia also is called the Mother of Presidents. The state was once home to eight presidents of the United States. George Washington, Thomas Jefferson, James Madison, and James Monroe were born there. William Henry Harrison, John Tyler, Zachary Taylor, and Woodrow Wilson also were born in Virginia.

James Monroe served as governor of Virginia twice before he was elected president of the United States.

State Seal and Motto

Virginia adopted its state seal in 1776. It reminds Virginians of their state's government. The state seal stamped on government papers makes them official.

Virginia's seal shows a soldier holding a spear and a sword. The soldier is standing on a man whose crown has fallen off. The man stands for tyranny. Tyranny is unfair government. The seal shows Virginia's victory over tyranny.

Virginia was one of England's 13 colonies. The colonists thought the English were unfair rulers. The colonists fought for their freedom during the Revolutionary War (1775–1783). Virginia's seal stands for the colonists' victory over the English.

Virginia's motto is on its state seal. The state's official motto is "Thus always to tyrants." The state motto means freedom is important to Virginians. They will fight unfair rulers.

Virginia's seal stands for victory over tyranny. Virginians helped defeat England during the Revolutionary War.

State Capitol and Flag

The state capitol building is in Richmond. Richmond is Virginia's capital city. Virginia's state government meets in the capital city.

Thomas Jefferson designed the capitol building to look like an ancient Roman temple built in France. Builders completed the capitol in 1792. Some people believe Virginia's capitol was the first modern building with this design.

Richmond was the capital of the Confederate States of America during the Civil War (1861–1865). The Confederacy's government met in Virginia's capitol. Most of the buildings in Richmond were destroyed during the Civil War. The capitol was one of the few buildings left standing.

Virginia's government adopted the state flag in 1776. The flag is dark blue with the state seal located in the center.

Virginia's state government has met in the capitol building in Richmond for more than 200 years.

State Bird

The northern cardinal became Virginia's state bird in 1950. People in Virginia once called the cardinal the Virginia nightingale. Virginians thought the cardinal sounded like the nightingale.

Adult cardinals grow to be about 8 inches (20 centimeters) long. Male cardinals are bright red. Female cardinals are light brown. Both have a crest of red feathers on their heads.

Cardinals live in the eastern and northern United States. Cardinals do not migrate. They live in one place all year.

Cardinals build their nests in bushes and in trees. Cardinal eggs hatch in about 12 days. Both male and female cardinals care for their young.

The northern cardinal also is the state bird of Illinois, Indiana, Kentucky, North Carolina, Ohio, and West Virginia.

Male cardinals are bright red. They have black markings around their beaks.

State Tree

The American dogwood tree became Virginia's state tree in 1956. Dogwood trees grow in the eastern United States.

Dogwood trees are 20 to 35 feet (6 to 11 meters) tall. Their branches can reach 20 to 25 feet (6 to 7.5 meters) in length. But most dogwood trees are smaller and look like bushes.

Dogwood trees are deciduous. Their green leaves fall off in autumn and grow back in spring. Dogwood trees have a thick covering of leaves. The leaves provide a lot of shade.

In spring, dogwood trees bloom. White or pink blossoms appear on their branches. Many people like the dogwood's sweet-smelling blossoms. Some Virginians plant dogwood trees in their yards.

American dogwood trees grow on the capitol grounds in Richmond. Their blossoms can be white or pink.

State Flower

Government officials made the American dogwood tree blossom the state flower in 1918.

Dogwood blossoms have four white or pink bracts. Many people think these brightly colored leaves are petals. But they are not. Dogwood blossoms have no petals.

The four bracts on a dogwood blossom surround a small green center. A cluster of red berries grows from the center in autumn. Birds, squirrels, and caterpillars eat the brightly colored dogwood berries. But people should not eat the berries. They may get sick.

Dogwood berries contain quinine. Quinine can be used to make medicine that reduces fevers. People also use dogwood berries to make red dyes. The dyes can be used to color clothing.

Dogwood blossoms have a green center surrounded by four brightly colored bracts.

State Dog

The American foxhound became Virginia's state dog in 1966. American foxhounds are tan, black, and white. These medium-sized dogs can grow up to 2 feet (.6 meters) tall. American foxhounds weigh up to 70 pounds (32 kilograms).

Hunters gave American foxhounds their name. The dogs have a strong sense of smell that helps them track foxes. Foxhunting was a popular sport among Virginia's colonists. Today, some Virginians still use American foxhounds to hunt foxes. A group of 15 to 20 dogs will follow a fox's trail. Hunters will ride on horses behind the dogs.

Some people keep American foxhounds as pets. But these dogs need a great deal of exercise. They enjoy living in rural areas where their owners can let them run. American foxhounds also need to be around other dogs. They can become lonely without their company.

American foxhounds still are used to hunt foxes. Hunters often use many dogs to follow a fox's trail.

More State Symbols

State Boat: In 1988, officials chose the Chesapeake Bay deadrise as Virginia's state boat. Chesapeake Bay deadrises are wooden motor boats with small cabins. People mainly use these boats to catch fish from the Chesapeake Bay. The Chesapeake Bay is a narrow part of the Atlantic Ocean. The bay lies along the coast of Virginia.

State Fish: The brook trout became the state fish in 1993. This fish is a member of the salmon family. The brook trout lives in clear, cold streams in Virginia.

State Insect: The tiger swallowtail butterfly is one of Virginia's newest state symbols. Virginians chose it as the state insect in 1991. This butterfly has yellow and black stripes on its wings.

State Shell: The oyster shell became the state shell in 1974. Oysters live at the bottoms of the Atlantic and Pacific Oceans. Some Virginians use nets to catch oysters from boats.

The tiger-striped wings of a tiger swallowtail butterfly make it easy to spot.

Places to Visit

Colonial Williamsburg

Williamsburg is in southeastern Virginia. This town was Virginia's capital from 1699 to 1780. Today, Williamsburg looks much as it did 200 years ago. Visitors see actors recreate everyday colonial life. Visitors also can participate in these recreations and talk to the actors.

Luray Caverns

The Luray Caverns are near the town of Luray. Water formed these caves more than 400 million years ago. Colorful rock formations continue to grow inside the caverns. Water drips from the ceiling of the caverns. Minerals in the water build up and create rock formations.

The Mariners' Museum

The Mariners' Museum is in Newport News. Museum visitors learn the history of traveling the world's oceans. The museum features model ships and working steam engines. Figureheads from old ships are displayed. These giant wooden carvings once decorated the fronts of ships.

Words to Know

bract (BRAKT)—a colorful leaf; dogwood blossoms have four bracts that look like petals.

Confederacy (con-FED-ur-a-see)—the group of 11 Southern states that left the United States in 1861; the Confederate States of America

crest (KREST)—a crown of feathers on a bird's head

deciduous (di-SIJ-oo-uhss)—a tree that sheds its leaves in the fall; leaves on deciduous trees grow back in the spring.

dominion (duh-MIN-yuhn)—a colony that is allowed to govern itself; Virginia was an English dominion.

migrate (MYE-grate)—to move from one place to another when seasons change or when food is scarce

tyranny (TEER-uh-nee)—the unfair use of power by a government

Read More

Capstone Press Geography Department. *Virginia.* One Nation. Mankato, Minn.: Capstone Press, 1997.

Fradin, Dennis B. *Virginia.* From Sea to Shining Sea. Chicago: Children's Press, 1992.

Thompson, Kathleen. *Virginia.* Portrait of America. Austin, Texas: Raintree Steck-Vaughn, 1996.

Useful Addresses

Secretary of the
  Commonwealth
  of Virginia
P.O. Box 2454
Richmond, VA 23218

Virginia Historical Society
428 North Boulevard
Richmond, VA 23220

Internet Sites

Colonial Williamsburg Foundation
http://www.history.org
Virginia Historical Society
http://www.vahistorical.org
Virginia! Welcome to the Commonwealth
http://www.state.va.us

Index